Have You Seen Houses?

by Joanne Oppenheim

Young Scott Books

All Rights Reserved.
Text © 1973 by Joanne Oppenheim.

Published by Young Scott Books, a Division of the
Addison-Wesley Publishing Company, Inc., Reading, Mass. 01867.

Library of Congress Cataloging in Publication Data
Oppenheim, Joanne.
Have you seen houses?
SUMMARY: Describes in verse the different kinds
of houses people live in throughout the world.
1. Dwellings—Juvenile literature. [1. Dwellings]
I. Title.
GT171.066   301.5′4   72-11542
ISBN 0-201-09300-6

Credits—
Have You Seen Houses?

apartments—DPI Jules Zalon
look-alike houses—L.M. Kendall
FPG Weldon King
people gather together—The Public Archives of Canada
Harold M. Lambert
farm house—United Press International
mountain house—Englehard
built in the past—Sleepy Hollow Restorations
splendiferous houses—Travel & Promotion Division
Dept. of Conservation & Development
Raleigh, North Carolina
tents—FPG Julien H. Bryan
ALPHA
trailer—FPG John Gajda
sampans—DPI Harold S. Jacobs
FPG Konran/Media, Inc.
aquanauts—NASA
a house built on stilts—SEF
northern houses—State of Massachusetts
chiseled from rocks—National Park Service
reeds and leaves—Safari Productions Inc.
piece by piece—Anthony Oppenheim
bought to be brought all complete—Infinity Photography
geodesic dome—Geodesic Structures, Inc.
White House—Washington Convention and Visitors Bureau

Have you seen houses?

Tall or small

high or low

in a stack

or in a row

urban

suburban

a city

a town

side by side

or up and down.

Apartments
compartments
apart and complete
with spaces to sleep
and places to eat.

One room
two rooms
sometimes many more
people living on every floor.

Good neighbors
kind neighbors
some you only greet
noisy neighbors
nosy neighbors
some you never meet.

Upstairs neighbors
downstairs neighbors
neighbors down the halls
but they all share one roof
and the outside walls.

Now look at these look-alike houses in rows
on look-alike streets...
Have you ever seen those?

Except for the number
except for the name
the outside of each is exactly the same!

But inside
each house has a look of its own
its own kind of clutter and color and tone.

Noisy or quiet

messy or neat

the people inside make each house unique.

But outside

the look-alike houses in rows

all look-alike...

Have you ever seen those?

Most people gather together to live

to buy

to sell

to get

to give.

Together for work

together for play

till rush hour comes at the end of each day.

Then everyone rushes to get to their home

a house or apartment

a place of their own!

But some people long for the wide-open spaces
with acres and acres of neighborless spaces!

With cows

and sows

to milk and feed

with plants in fields

to seed

and weed

with crops to cut

and flocks to tend

farm days are full from end to end.

If it weren't for farm families

who live mostly alone

we'd all have to grow

food of our own.

Here is a house aloft and alone.
If you go see your neighbor
you're far
far
from home.

No need for fences...
just think of the view.
But... if you run out of sugar...
just what
do you do?

Built in the past

built to last

long ago

with attic on top

and cellar

below

with crannies

and nooks

and places to hide

with porches for rocking

when it's too hot inside.

How many people have lived here before?

How many names have been heard at the door?

How many footsteps have crossed every floor?

But the old house stands ready

still ready

for more.

Locked behind walls
with turrets and towers
locked behind gates
to keep out the prowlers
ringed with a fence, a hedge, or a moat
splendiferous houses are often remote.

But with so many rooms
if you played hide-and-seek
you might not be found
for more than a week!

Have you seen houses
for people who roam
for people who travel
but never leave home?

Here are houses for people who move with the seasons
to farm or to hunt — they move for such reasons.
North, east, south, or westward they roam
wherever they move they move with their home.

A tent they can pitch
a tent they can pack
a tent that can travel
on somebody's back.

Now people travel
with houses that move...
they travel for fun and
not to hunt food.

A house that can move
should you want to go far.
You live like a turtle
your feet are your car.

The forest is waiting
the lakeside
the shore.
No need to leave home
you just move your door!

Here is a house
or is it a boat?
A home for the water
a home that can float.

From sampan to sampan these houseboats are tied
like houses on streets that are built side by side
except with this house you can ride with the tide.
You can choose a new neighbor by taking a ride...
or if you prefer a life more remote
you can leave the whole fleet when you live on a boat.

No need to go shopping—your dinner's below—
just catch it and cook it wherever you go!

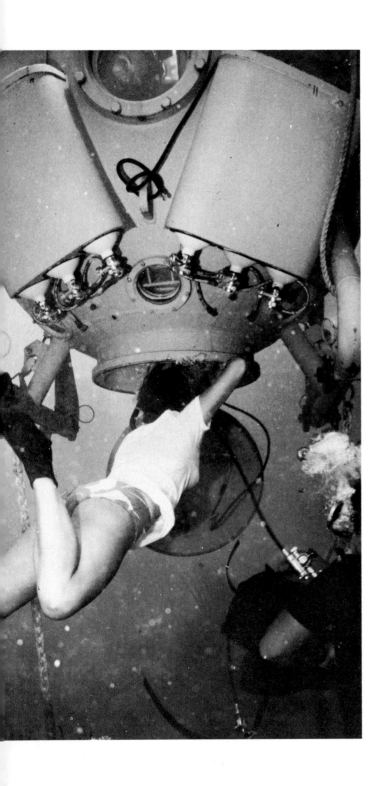

Astronauts
aquanauts
dare to explore
places that no one has been to before.

People exploring
above
or below
need houses to live in
wherever they go.

Whether your neighbor is

near or far

in city

or town

wherever you are . . .

whether your house

can travel or not

whether the weather

is frigid or hot

whatever the weather

wherever you go

whether you live

in the heat

or the snow —

all houses are built

to keep people dry

out of the cold

or the heat of the sky.

Near the equator where bananas grow
they never have blizzards and never see snow.
So people build huts of bamboo or leaves
to weather the heat and to let in the breeze.

A house built on stilts can keep people dry
when tropical rains make the river run high.

A house built on stilts can keep out the prowlers—
especially wild prowlers
that tend to be growlers!

While far to the north where the winter winds whip
people build houses with thick walls of brick.

Let the wind
huff and puff and blow!

Let there be
ice and sleet and snow!

Where the wind bites hard
with snow and with sleet
this is a house
to keep in the heat!

Chiseled from rocks

chopped from trees

sun-baked mud

reeds and leaves

people build houses from

what they have found

these houses were built

with gifts from the ground.

A house can be built piece by piece
on a lot
or
bought to be brought all complete
to the spot!

Houses together

houses alone

houses for rent

houses to own

houses of brick

or wood

or stone.

Houses in cities

houses in town

side by side

or up and down

bi-level

split level

geodesic dome ·

wherever you live . . .

Your house is your home!

Styles of Houses throughout the Ages:

A Brief Survey by
Frank O. Braynard

PRE HISTORY:

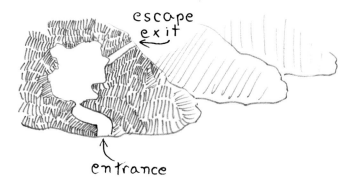

Cave with many rooms — about 500,000 B.C.

EUROPEAN:

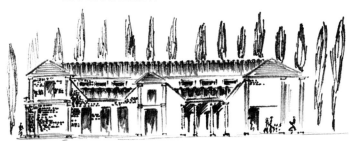

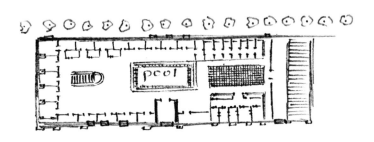

House of Pansa, Rome — 10 A.D.

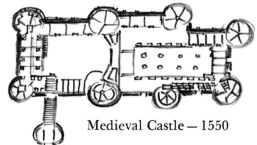

Medieval Castle — 1550

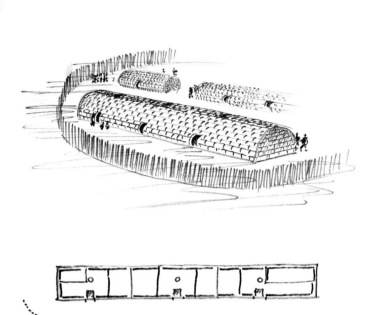

Iroquois Long House — 1,000 B.C.

Mesa Verde cliff ruins — 800 A.D.

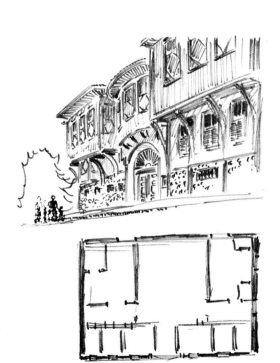

Town House — Constantinople 1500

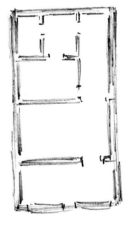

Flemish town house — 1600

UNITED STATES:

Settler's Log Cabin — 1700

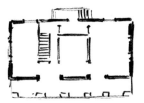

Southern Mansion, St. Martinsville, La. — 1800

PACIFIC:

Batak Village, Sumatra — 15th Century

ASIAN:

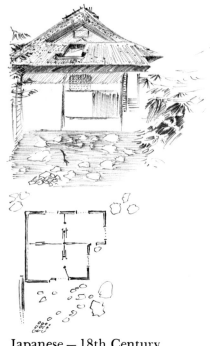

Japanese — 18th Century

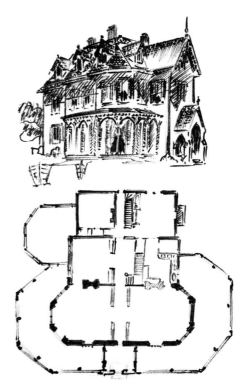

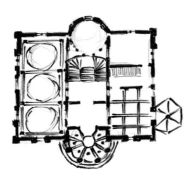

Greek Revival in N.Y. — 1848

Midwest Victorian — 1860

AFRICAN:

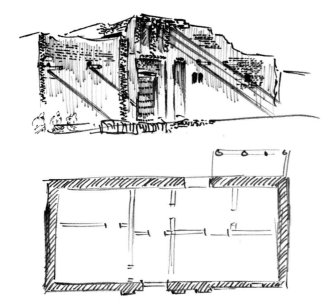

Timbuktu mud house — 19th Century

Zulu dwelling — 19th Century